W9-DGF-341

The
SECRET
WORLD
of the
FLOWER
FAIRIES

The SECRET WORLD of the FLOWER FAIRIES

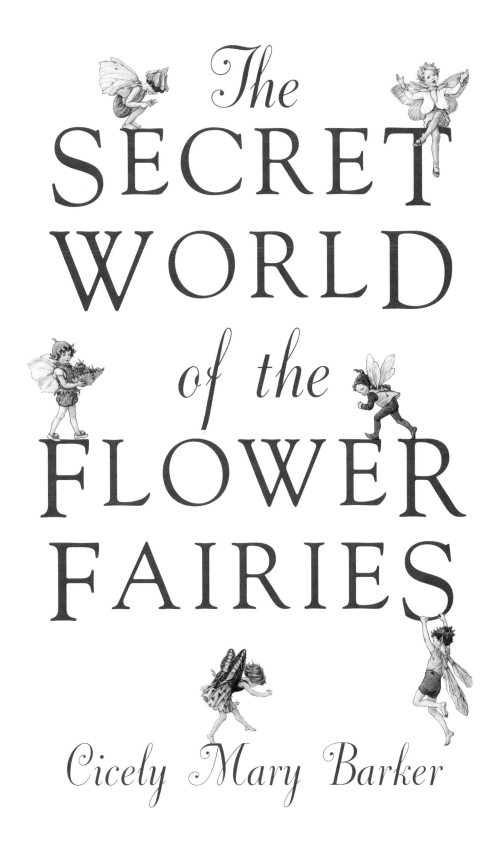

Cicely Mary Barker

FREDERICK WARNE

The reproductions in this book have been made using the most modern electronic scanning methods from entirely new transparencies of Cicely Mary Barker's original watercolours. They enable Cicely Mary Barker's skill as an artist to be appreciated as never before.

FREDERICK WARNE

Published by the Penguin Group
Penguin Books Ltd, 27 Wrights Lane, London W8 5TZ, England
Penguin Putnam Inc., 375 Hudson Street, New York, NY 10014, USA
Penguin Books Australia Ltd, Ringwood, Victoria, Australia
Penguin Books Canada Ltd, 10 Alcorn Avenue, Toronto, Ontario, Canada M4V 3B2
Penguin Books (N.Z.) Ltd, 182-190 Wairau Road, Auckland 10, New Zealand

Penguin Books Ltd, Registered Offices: Harmondsworth, Middlesex, England

First published in 1998

ISBN 0 7232 4457 X

Colour reproduction by Saxon Photolitho Ltd, Norwich
Printed and bound in Great Britain by William Clowes Limited, Beccles and London

CONTENTS

~✳~

Introduction to the Flower Fairies

$\mathcal{D}$id you know that in your garden, in between the neat borders and blooming beds, lives a bustling community of Flower Fairies? In every wood, meadow and hedgerow, hundreds of invisible Flower Fairies work and play. Unseen by human eyes, these tiny fairies wax glossy plant leaves and ensure that flower petals radiate with lustrous colour. Nature sprites who care for flowers and trees, the Flower Fairies are named for the particular plant that they nurture. Although some plants only flower for a few weeks of the year, Flower Fairies are busy year-round helping their friends. Just a single, magical touch from a Flower Fairy can revive a wilting, sickly plant. The fairies spend much of their time sowing, for whenever a seed is planted a new fairy springs to life.

$\mathcal{S}$hy, secretive creatures, Flower Fairies look like beautiful human children, but with pointy, elfin ears, dreamy eyes and wings like a butterfly's. Fairies come in all shapes and sizes, but the Flower Fairies are amongst the smallest of all fairies, ranging in height from four inches to six inches (10 cm to 15 cm).

The Winter Aconite Fairy

An aura of grace and beauty surrounds the Flower Fairies, and they charm any person who beholds them. A mixture of nice and naughty fairies populate the fairy world, but most Flower Fairies use their powers to do good. Like nature itself, however, Flower Fairies can be temperamental. Though they are usually loving and friendly, they also have moods of sadness and spite.

Flower Fairies are fond of humans, but they prefer to remain invisible when people approach. Few people have ever seen fairies, but that does not prove that they do not exist. Since the Middle Ages, favoured humans all over the world have recounted their contact with fairies. These accounts vary, for fairyland appears and disappears according to the whims of its residents. Eyewitnesses, however, offer rich, evocative descriptions of their elusive encounters with fairies which help us to envisage their idyllic, hidden world. In the pages that follow, you will learn about every aspect of fairy life—from their homes and jobs, to their dazzling courts and spectacular balls. So, leave your disbelief behind, and prepare to enter the secret world of the Flower Fairies. Ssssshhhh! Don't disturb the fairies. . .

The Black Bryony Fairy

The Blackthorn Fairy

The Fairy Code

*F*airies hold certain values in high esteem, and these ten attributes comprise the Fairy Code. Even the naughtiest fairies abide by these rules in their dealings with other fairies, though not necessarily when interacting with humans. If you, too, follow the Fairy Code, you will increase your chances of befriending fairies and avoid offending these sensitive creatures.

THE FAIRY CODE

* cheerfulness
* generosity
* neatness
* honesty
* politeness
* secrecy
* beauty
* kindness
* diligence
* sense of humour

*H*umans who honour the Fairy Code may reap rewards, but wise people accept fairy gifts with caution. Never thank a fairy directly, for they consider it insulting. Instead, bow politely and leave dainty offerings where the fairies will find them. Above all, never reveal the source of a fairy gift. Fairies cannot tolerate indiscretion and will certainly revoke the gift. Valuing generosity, fairies begrudge any people unwilling to share. Fairies do not ask before taking, but they unfailingly repay loans with generous interest. If you borrow from a fairy, only return exactly what you borrowed. Any more or less will insult the fairy.

Where are the Flower Fairies?

Wherever there are flowers, there are sure to be Flower Fairies close by. Nobody knows quite how many fairies exist today. Modern life threatens nature and has caused fairy numbers to dwindle. Finding Flower Fairies will be difficult, but understanding how fairies think and behave will simplify the task. Most importantly, you must let your imagination guide you to the Flower Fairies and truly believe that they exist. Fairies can detect even a shadow of doubt and will remain resolutely invisible. Not everyone can see fairies. You can search high and low, but if the fairies do not favour you they will not appear. Throughout history, children, poets, artists and lovers have had the most contact with fairies. Even if your search does not succeed, take comfort in the knowledge that you have been in the company of fairies. Curious creatures, Flower Fairies enjoy spying on humans!

Fairies cast a spell of glamour, or fairy enchantment, over mortals' senses to prevent them from seeing fairies. If they so desire, however, fairies can reveal themselves to humans. In special circumstances, fairies apply fairy ointment to humans' eyes, which allows them to glimpse the invisible fairy world.

There are also certain means and times conducive to catching fairies unawares. Look for fairies at noon, midnight, dusk or dawn. Most reported fairy sightings occur at these transition times. When engrossed in a difficult task or frolicking with wild abandon, fairies drop their defences and become visible to humans. If you espy an unsuspecting fairy, be sure to stay very quiet and avoid detection. Never look for fairies in a group, as it will be a fruitless pursuit.

Take extreme caution if you plan to search for fairies. If caught snooping in a fairy home, you will suffer harsh penalties. Humans who visit fairyland pass the rest of their days pining away and searching in vain for a way back. A person taken captive by fairies, however, cannot escape without the help of a kind fairy. Fairies punish infringements of privacy with an onslaught of sharp pinches. In extreme cases, trespassers have been blinded by vengeful fairies. Though kind and mild, Flower Fairies take exception to humans plucking rare flowers, chopping down trees and eating unripe fruits and nuts. They punish wrongdoers with stomach aches, weeds and wilting crops.

Tips for Finding Fairies

❀ Touch a rock with the correct number of primroses in a posy and fairyland will open for you. Take heed, for placing the wrong number of primroses spells doom. The fairies will know you seek access and will take revenge.

❀ Walk around a hill nine times under a full moon and you will find yourself at the fairy market.

❀ Stale bread carried in your pocket wards off fairy mischief. If you wish to see fairies, do not have even a breadcrumb on your person.

❀ Look around thorn trees, which often conceal the door to a fairy residence. Remember, fairies wish to deter intruders and will not welcome you if you crash through the brambles.

❀ Cold iron terrifies all fairies. A pair of shears or a horseshoe placed in your garden is sure to drive the Flower Fairies away.

❀ Salt keeps fairies at bay. It stings their delicate fingers and lips.

* Four leaf clover, the main ingredient in fairy ointment, dissolves glamour and allows humans to see fairies. This powerful plant also provides the power to grant wishes.

* Gaze at fairies calmly and steadily. Looking away or blinking gives a fairy enough time to escape.

* Daisy chains and crowns prevent children from being carried away by evil fairies. Other plants, such as ground ivy, St. John's wort, rowan and mountain ash offer protection against fairy harm.

* Find a fairy possession, such as a tiny jacket or reed pipe, and the owner will eventually appear before you and implore you to give it back.

* Do not look for fairies around loud clanging noises, such as deep church bells or noisy machinery, for these sounds pain sensitive fairy ears.

* Running water frightens many fairies, so do not look for fairies along riverbanks or near hose-pipes.

The Fairy Court

When you dream of a fairy court, what do you picture? Do you imagine a luxurious castle decorated with tapestries, crystal chandeliers and gold thrones? Then you would get quite a surprise should you glimpse a fairy palace! Wonders to behold, the beautiful Flower Fairy courts are entirely furnished by nature. The kings and queens sit on simple toadstool thrones and rest their dainty feet on poplar fluff cushions. A veil of fairy dust hangs over the court, making the flowers and trees within twinkle and shine with magic. Fairy courts are the inner-most sanctums of the fairy realm, so if you should encounter one be sure not to gawk. Discreet observers might be tolerated, but an obvious intruder would suffer severe punishment.

Flower Fairies live in hierarchical societies governed by kings and queens. These benevolent sovereigns rule wisely over their subjects, ensuring that the fairies dwell harmoniously together and settling any disputes that arise. The fairy monarchs recognise that each fairy performs an

The Chicory Fairy

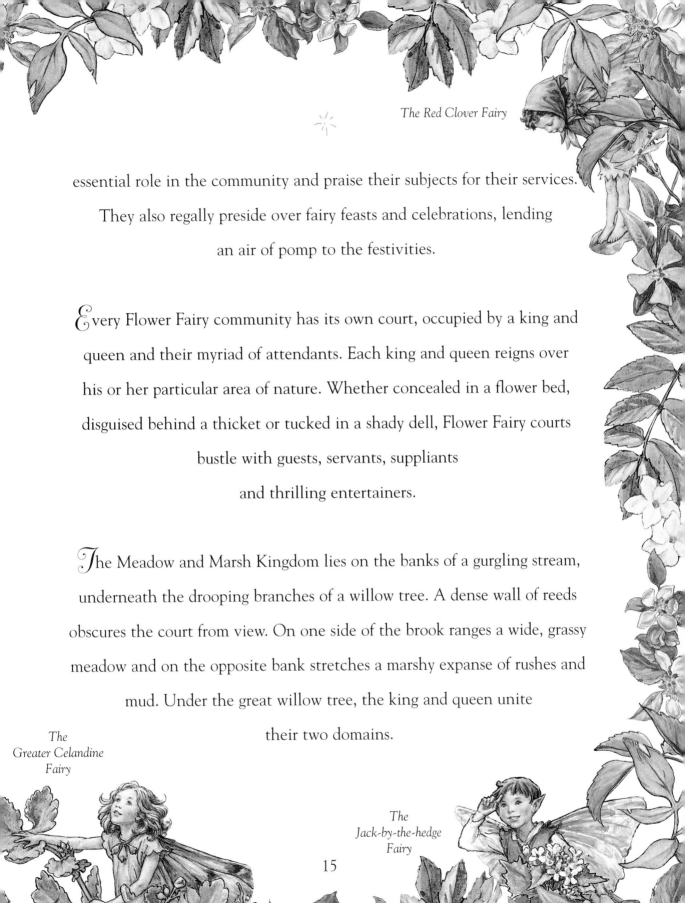

The Red Clover Fairy

essential role in the community and praise their subjects for their services. They also regally preside over fairy feasts and celebrations, lending an air of pomp to the festivities.

Every Flower Fairy community has its own court, occupied by a king and queen and their myriad of attendants. Each king and queen reigns over his or her particular area of nature. Whether concealed in a flower bed, disguised behind a thicket or tucked in a shady dell, Flower Fairy courts bustle with guests, servants, suppliants and thrilling entertainers.

The Meadow and Marsh Kingdom lies on the banks of a gurgling stream, underneath the drooping branches of a willow tree. A dense wall of reeds obscures the court from view. On one side of the brook ranges a wide, grassy meadow and on the opposite bank stretches a marshy expanse of rushes and mud. Under the great willow tree, the king and queen unite their two domains.

*The
Greater Celandine
Fairy*

*The
Jack-by-the-hedge
Fairy*

The King of the Marshes, the *Kingcup Fairy* rules fairly and justly. Elegant in his golden crown and velvety green cloak, he proudly lords over the fairy treasure. Have you ever heard of fairy gold? The fairies do not keep a cache of heavy coins. Instead, they hoard the *Kingcup Fairy's* shining cups of gold. Little elves come to admire the golden chalices gleaming in the marshes. They guard their king's treasure fiercely and punish human trespassers who plunder his wealth. Intruders who disrespectfully gather armfuls of yellow flowers might lose a shoe or boot in the muddy morass. Though the *Kingcup Fairy* radiates grandeur, he deigns to speak with even his lowliest subjects and listens attentively to their needs. The marsh fairies revere their noble leader and cheer when he ventures out of the fairy court.

The Kingcup Fairy

16

*E*nthroned amongst her lacy, white flowers, the *Queen of the Meadow Fairy* reigns gently over the Flower Fairies who abide in the fields and the creatures who dwell in the swampy pools. The silvery minnows swimming in the stream and the kingfishers nesting in the willow tree are all her loyal servants. Whenever she calls, her courtiers hurry to do their queen's bidding. Dutiful dragonflies and frogs fly or hop to carry out their royal errands. The *Queen of the Meadow Fairy* wears a necklace of white flowers, but no fancy tiara crowns her head. So stately is her manner that she has no need for outward signs to show her majesty. No one who beholds the *Queen of the Meadow Fairy* can mistake the regal air about her.

*The
Queen of the Meadow
Fairy*

*The
Strawberry
Fairy*

17

The little *Buttercup Fairy* is the Princess of the Meadow Kingdom. Like the king she has a wealth of gold, glossy cups, but her little flowers are the royal family's gift to the residents of the meadows and marshes. The *Buttercup Fairy* spreads her array of riches under the summer sky and offers them to anyone who wishes to pick. A sweet, generous fairy, she charms all visitors to the court with her warm smile and chiming laugh. If children hold buttercups under their chin, the *Buttercup Fairy* might grant their wishes.

Iris

Some Flower Fairies reside permanently at the court, serving as companions and servants to their king and queen. The faithful *Iris Fairy* acts as the queen's lady-in-waiting. She brushes her mistress's fluffy hair, bathes her with cool, clear water from the stream and helps her to dress for formal events. When they take long walks through the marshes together, the queen confides all her secrets and worries in the trusted attendant who follows her like a bright, yellow shadow.

*E*very fairy court houses numerous courtiers. The *Periwinkle Fairy* willingly accompanies the king on diplomatic trips and sporting excursions. Although the king and his valet laugh together, the *Periwinkle Fairy* always respects his master. A gallant knight, he would defend his king's honour to the death. Any mission the king charges him with he zealously performs. Before departing on his courageous crusades through the murkiest swamps, he kneels and offers the queen a blossom as a token of remembrance.

When the king and queen parade through their kingdom, the *Agrimony Fairies* march at the front of the procession. Standing straight and tall, they solemnly carry spikes of burrs like miniature soldiers. Obedient page-boys, the *Agrimony Fairies* serve their monarchs by proclaiming royal decrees, delivering messages and swiftly running errands. These smart little envoys announce their presence with a call on a honeysuckle trumpet and proudly represent the fairy court throughout the realm.

Dressed in prickly armour, the *Greater Knapweed Fairy* guards the entrance to the fairy court. He holds a sharp stalk of knapweed and vigilantly patrols underneath the willow tree. The tireless sentry of the king and queen's safety, he scours the court for signs of intruders. All callers at the court must first gain the *Greater Knapweed Fairy's* approval. Although he wouldn't like you to know it, underneath his spiky uniform the *Greater Knapweed Fairy* is mild and kind.

When the king and queen hold court, their subjects come to pay homage. The humble subjects curtsy and bear offerings of ripe, wild berries or fragrant bouquets. With a blast of fanfare the beautiful *Wild Rose Fairy*, the Queen of the Hedgerow, floats into the court. Little servant elves strew a carpet of petals along the visiting dignitary's path. Rulers of other kingdoms often pay goodwill visits to neighbouring realms, to keep relationships between all Flower Fairies friendly and cooperative.

The Wild Rose Fairy

The Greater Knapweed Fairy

The *Wild Rose Fairy* brings a present of rose hip tea for the meadow and marsh community to enjoy and sits upon an honorary throne next to her hosts.

The Elderberry Fairy

*N*ot all the Flower Fairies visiting the court come to bring gifts. Although the fairies usually get along peacefully, occasional quibbles erupt between neighbours and colleagues. As the king and queen listen patiently, a suppliant complains that weeds always strangle her flowers. The two rulers work out a compromise that allows both weeds and flowers to thrive. Next, the *Elderberry Fairy* implores the queen to negotiate with the birds, for they are eating too many berries. Other fairies ask for relief and the monarchs assign helpers to assist with their chores.

*N*o Flower Fairy court lacks for entertainment. The king and queen welcome wandering minstrels into their home and the court reverberates with the sound of music and dancing. The *Holly Fairy*, a roving jester with bells on his hat and shoes, tours the Flower Fairy courts. Dazzling his regal audience with amazing juggling displays, he capers and clowns until the king and queen ache from laughter.

The Holly Fairy

23

Homes and Housekeeping

It is futile to search for a fairy house, as Flower Fairies rarely live anywhere that you would find them. Shy and private creatures, they make cosy homes in remote undergrowth or in hidden dells covered with brambles to deter intruders. Fairies guard their privacy fiercely and do their utmost to avoid prying human eyes. Humans who accidentally stumble upon fairy homes often suffer dire consequences. Unfortunate trespassers are sometimes struck dumb so that they cannot reveal the location of a fairy community. After all, wouldn't you be angry if a giant foot crashed down upon your roof? If you do come across a fairy home unawares, leave it undisturbed and pretend that you haven't noticed it.

A typical fairy home has a velvety carpet of soft, green moss. Flower Fairies hang up lacy curtains made from silky cobwebs which float gently on the breeze. These gossamer drapes keep insects out of the home and are cleaned every

The Willow-Catkin Fairy

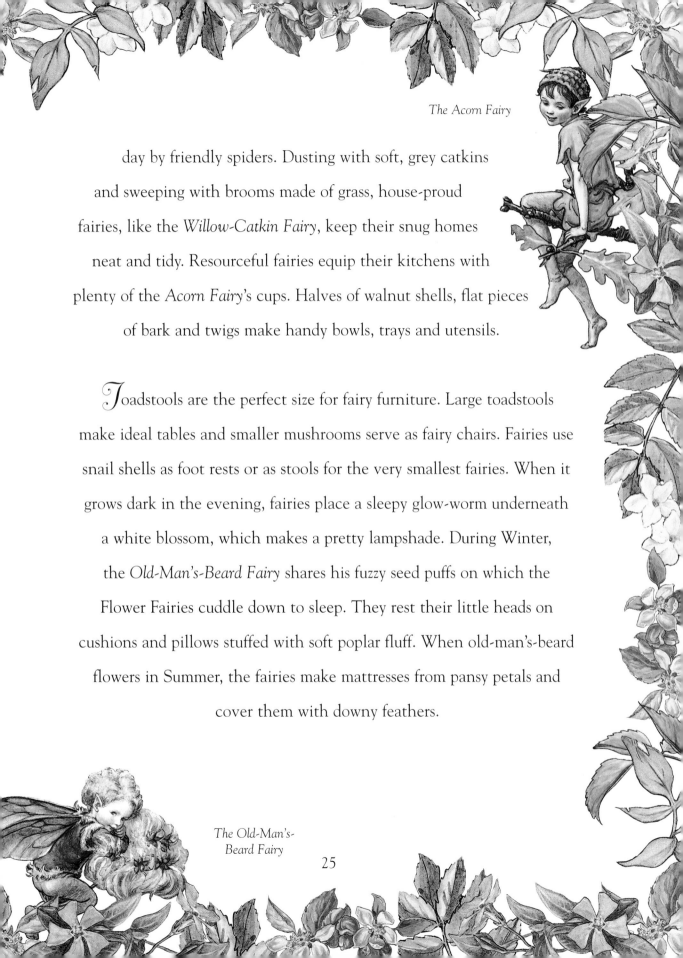

day by friendly spiders. Dusting with soft, grey catkins and sweeping with brooms made of grass, house-proud fairies, like the *Willow-Catkin Fairy*, keep their snug homes neat and tidy. Resourceful fairies equip their kitchens with plenty of the *Acorn Fairy*'s cups. Halves of walnut shells, flat pieces of bark and twigs make handy bowls, trays and utensils.

Toadstools are the perfect size for fairy furniture. Large toadstools make ideal tables and smaller mushrooms serve as fairy chairs. Fairies use snail shells as foot rests or as stools for the very smallest fairies. When it grows dark in the evening, fairies place a sleepy glow-worm underneath a white blossom, which makes a pretty lampshade. During Winter, the *Old-Man's-Beard Fairy* shares his fuzzy seed puffs on which the Flower Fairies cuddle down to sleep. They rest their little heads on cushions and pillows stuffed with soft poplar fluff. When old-man's-beard flowers in Summer, the fairies make mattresses from pansy petals and cover them with downy feathers.

*The Old-Man's-
Beard Fairy*

*F*lower Fairies, like their friends the magpies, gravitate towards anything colourful, shiny or sparkling. They decorate their homes with smooth pink pebbles, glossy horse chestnuts and glittering crystals. Strewn around fairy homes, garlands of seasonal flowers hide the dwellings from view and scent the air with sweet perfume. In Autumn, fairies deck their homes with glorious wreaths and ropes of the *White Bryony Fairy*'s red berries. Their most valuable treasures include human objects that they have pilfered from the wayside: shiny copper pennies, milky glass marbles and pretty buttons are proudly displayed in fairy homes.

The White Bryony Fairy

26

Fairies make their homes in secluded places, sheltered from the sky by leaves and branches. When it rains, the *Nasturtium Fairy* hands out leaves for the fairies to use as umbrellas. They do not mind getting a bit wet, because they know that the showers will wash their homes clean. Although garden fairies prefer to live in cosy homes hidden amongst the flower beds, countryside fairies are nomads. Fairies such as the *Wayfaring Tree Fairy* stay on the move and simply nestle under a leaf when they need to sleep.

The Nasturtium Fairy

The Wayfaring Tree Fairy

Jobs

~ ✳ ~

As you know, each Flower Fairy cares for one variety of flower or tree. Even when their particular flower is not in season the Flower Fairies assist their neighbours with gardening chores. However, the Flower Fairies have other needs, such as food and clothing. They require teachers for their young and a nurse for the sick. Just as in human towns, Flower Fairies with special talents provide important services for their communities.

The Flower Fairies have little need for a police force. Although they are mischievous and playful, the Flower Fairies love order. However, a brigade of watchmen guards the Flower Fairy community from menacing intruders who threaten the harmony of the fairy world.

The Dogwood Fairy

The Rush-Grass and Cotton-Grass Fairies

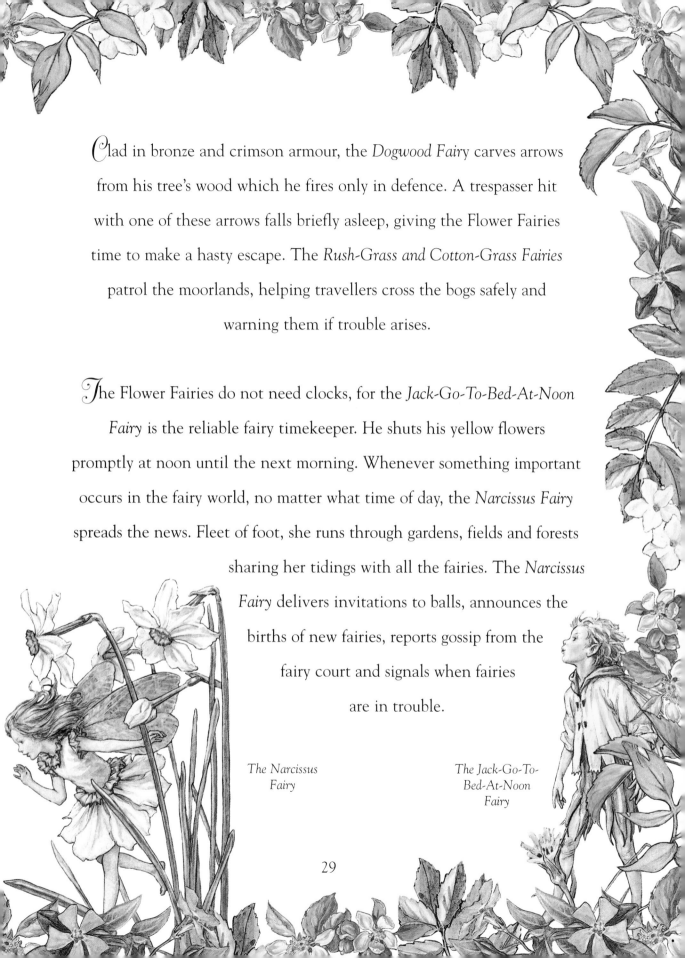

Clad in bronze and crimson armour, the *Dogwood Fairy* carves arrows from his tree's wood which he fires only in defence. A trespasser hit with one of these arrows falls briefly asleep, giving the Flower Fairies time to make a hasty escape. The *Rush-Grass and Cotton-Grass Fairies* patrol the moorlands, helping travellers cross the bogs safely and warning them if trouble arises.

The Flower Fairies do not need clocks, for the *Jack-Go-To-Bed-At-Noon Fairy* is the reliable fairy timekeeper. He shuts his yellow flowers promptly at noon until the next morning. Whenever something important occurs in the fairy world, no matter what time of day, the *Narcissus Fairy* spreads the news. Fleet of foot, she runs through gardens, fields and forests sharing her tidings with all the fairies. The *Narcissus Fairy* delivers invitations to balls, announces the births of new fairies, reports gossip from the fairy court and signals when fairies are in trouble.

The Narcissus Fairy

The Jack-Go-To-Bed-At-Noon Fairy

The Seamstress

Who sews buttons on to green elfin jackets? Who darns pixies' tiny socks? Who mends fairies' fancy frocks? The *Tansy Fairy* is the seamstress to the fairy world. With a needle from a pine tree and fine blades of grass for thread, she neatly stitches minuscule seams that only fairy eyes can see. Her exquisite embroidery produces everything from delicate handkerchiefs to luxurious quilts lined with thistledown. When the Flower Fairies need new clothes to wear, they bring their colourful petals and leaves to the *Tansy Fairy* and she turns them into a pretty dress or a smart suit. They always know where to find her—sitting in a sunny field with her sewing basket, humming at her needlework.

The Laundress

(O)nce the *Tansy Fairy* has sewn new outfits for the Flower Fairies, how do they keep them clean and tidy? Fairies cannot abide anything dirty, especially not their dainty clothes! The *Lavender Fairy* runs the fairy laundry. First, she collects the fairies' washing baskets piled high with dresses, trousers, hankies and sheets. With her helpers the butterflies, she carries the loads of laundry to a nearby stream. There she washes the clothes with lavender-scented soap then wrings out the water. Along the bank of the stream, she strings a line between two purple spikes of lavender and hangs out the clothes in the warm breeze. When the sweet-smelling clothes are dry, she carefully folds them and delivers the garments to their owners.

The Nurse

When little elves have skinned their knees, when pixies have tummy aches from eating too many berries or when fairies have broken their gauzy wings, the *Self-Heal Fairy* makes them well again. The nurse to the fairy world, the *Self-Heal Fairy* uses her magical herb to heal ills and soothe pains. Her gentle touch as she bathes and bandages makes the fairies feel better at once. Holding her patients' hands, she murmurs comforting words and soon they are on the mend. Sick animals travel from far and wide for the *Self-Heal Fairy's* cure. Mice with injured tails, frogs with wounded legs and rabbits with painful paws are just some of the grateful creatures treated by the *Self-Heal Fairy*.

The Banker

There is plenty to buy at the fairy market, from baubles and bells to bowls and bags of sweets. But what currency do the fairies use to pay for their pretty purchases? The *Herb Twopence Fairy* acts as the fairy banker. Each round leaf of his plant is worth a penny in fairy money. The yellow flowers, called fairy sovereigns, are worth two pence each. This cautious, studious fairy spends his days counting and polishing the shiny leaves, which grow two-by-two along the plant's stem. A miser the fairy banker is not. He generously doles out equal amounts of his coins to each fairy, and ensures that his herb twopence keep growing. Thanks to the *Herb Twopence Fairy's* healthy fund of flowers, the Flower Fairies never want for money.

Herb Twopence

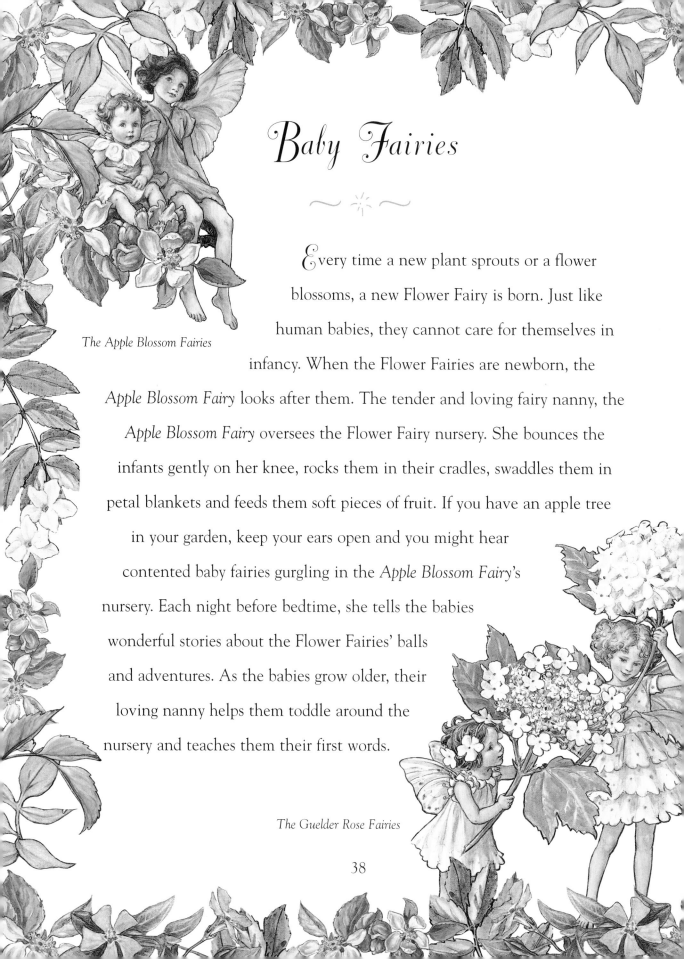

Baby Fairies

~ ✶ ~

The Apple Blossom Fairies

*E*very time a new plant sprouts or a flower blossoms, a new Flower Fairy is born. Just like human babies, they cannot care for themselves in infancy. When the Flower Fairies are newborn, the *Apple Blossom Fairy* looks after them. The tender and loving fairy nanny, the *Apple Blossom Fairy* oversees the Flower Fairy nursery. She bounces the infants gently on her knee, rocks them in their cradles, swaddles them in petal blankets and feeds them soft pieces of fruit. If you have an apple tree in your garden, keep your ears open and you might hear contented baby fairies gurgling in the *Apple Blossom Fairy's* nursery. Each night before bedtime, she tells the babies wonderful stories about the Flower Fairies' balls and adventures. As the babies grow older, their loving nanny helps them toddle around the nursery and teaches them their first words.

The Guelder Rose Fairies

38

When the babies can walk and speak, they attend the Flower Fairy school. Patient and calm, the *Black Medick Fairy* teaches the youngsters the ways of the fairy world. While the children sit on their toadstools, she instructs them on how to care for flowers, lectures them on the importance of sunshine and demonstrates how to weed and prune. With the help of her assistant, the *Guelder Rose Fairy*, she guides her eager pupils through gardens, fields and woods, naming all the different plants and answering the children's questions.

At playtime, the two teachers show the fledgling fairies how to use their gauzy little wings and practise fairy dances with them. After lunch, it's time for music lessons, when the class learns to sing traditional songs and play instruments. Perhaps the most important lesson that the students learn is how to impart their magic wisely. After spending a term at the fairy school, the young fairies graduate and begin to look after their own special flower or tree.

The Black Medick Fairies

Sheltered by the garden fence at the very back of the flower bed lies the
baby *Forget-Me-Not Fairy*. Kicking his plump little legs in the air, sucking his
thumb and quietly cooing, the infant *Forget-Me-Not Fairy* never cries.
He stares with wide-eyed wonder at the flowers around him and the clouds
in the sky. The other fairies never forget the adorable baby *Forget-Me-Not
Fairy*. They take it in turns to sing him lullabies and rock his cradle.

Up the trellis climbs a cluster of sweet peas with the *Sweet Pea Fairies* dwelling amongst their silky pods. The older *Sweet Pea Fairy* dotes on her little sister and fashions her charming baby bonnets. She also teaches the baby how to keep sweet pea tendrils curly and how to train the flowers to climb up the pergola. Once they finish their work at dawn, the *Sweet Pea Fairies* play dress-up and pat-a-cake until it is time for the baby fairy's nap.

The Fairy Market

~ ✳ ~

*O*nce a month, the inhabitants of the fairy world assemble by moonlight for the market. Humming with activity, the market hillside attracts all manner of fairies—from tiny elves and pixies, to trolls and imps, and of course, the Flower Fairies. At sunset, the traders flock to the grassy slope to set up their stalls and tents. They wear jingling bells on their clothes and fly bright flags to entice customers to the market. Some pedlars simply spread their wares out on a toadstool or a large leaf. Other vendors arrange their goods in fancy displays. Soon the air fills with the burble of merchants' patter, promising the best quality and prices to lure the fairies to their stalls.

*T*he Flower Fairies mount a pretty stall selling strings of berries, jars of bramble jam, baskets of fruit, jugs of dandelion wine and cowslip tea, trays of fairy cakes, fragrant bouquets and clothes sewn from petals. A flurry of shoppers crowds around the Flower Fairies' counter, fingering the soft garments and furtively sampling the ripe produce. Tattered and mud-bespattered, the *Mallow Fairy* hawks her seeds wrapped in leaves,

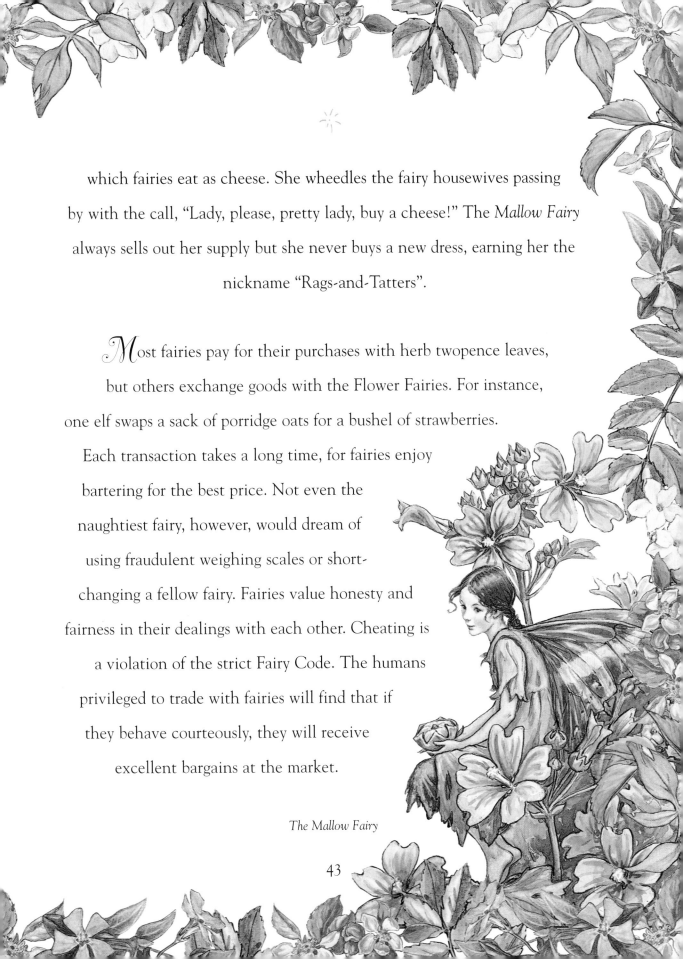

which fairies eat as cheese. She wheedles the fairy housewives passing by with the call, "Lady, please, pretty lady, buy a cheese!" The *Mallow Fairy* always sells out her supply but she never buys a new dress, earning her the nickname "Rags-and-Tatters".

Most fairies pay for their purchases with herb twopence leaves, but others exchange goods with the Flower Fairies. For instance, one elf swaps a sack of porridge oats for a bushel of strawberries. Each transaction takes a long time, for fairies enjoy bartering for the best price. Not even the naughtiest fairy, however, would dream of using fraudulent weighing scales or short-changing a fellow fairy. Fairies value honesty and fairness in their dealings with each other. Cheating is a violation of the strict Fairy Code. The humans privileged to trade with fairies will find that if they behave courteously, they will receive excellent bargains at the market.

The Mallow Fairy

When the Flower Fairies take breaks from minding their stall,
they eagerly browse around the market and examine the tempting array.
The baby fairies buy dolls carved from twigs and kites made from leaves and
lengths of spider-silk string. The older Flower Fairies purchase necessities
such as beeswax candles, lanolin soap, bags of fairy dust, magic wands and
gossamer patches for tattered wings. Fairy pedlars present a jumbled
collection of second-hand baubles, bric-a-brac, musical instruments
and even mice, moles and bats to keep as pets!

The Leprachauns run a busy booth, selling an assortment of shoes. Soft
slippers, sturdy boots, sandals and dancing shoes spill over the
table in every size and colour. The cobblers to the fairy world,
Leprachauns wear tri-cornered hats and little green jackets.
Even at the market, they carry on stitching soles and hammering heels.
Flower Fairies quickly wear out their footwear from all of their
dancing, so they flock to the Leprachauns' stall
to buy tiny new shoes.

Short, wrinkled, bearded Dwarves

work deep underground in precious metal mines.

They only emerge from the depths to take

their skilful handiwork to the fairy market.

Dwarves can never appear above

ground during daylight, which is why the

market is held at night. Their stall groans under

the weight of silver suits of armour,

necklaces, bangles, rings, metal treasure chests

and shiny bells. Attracted to the gleaming

silver, Flower Fairies buy trinkets

from the Dwarves.

$\mathcal{G}$oblins also toil in mines, digging for tin and then melting it down in their ferociously hot forge. These rather ugly, unpleasant fairies shape the heated tin into tools, utensils, bowls and plates. The Flower Fairies would prefer not to do business with the Goblins, but they need to purchase useful gardening tools, tankards and dishes made from tin.

$\mathcal{B}$rownies manage a popular food stall at the market. These ragged fairies dwell in homes and on farms. Asking for nothing from their human hosts but a bowl of cream and odd titbits, they clean the hearth, grind meal, thresh wheat and milk the cows. Though Brownies do not receive compensation for their labour, they often help themselves to excess milk, sugar and grain. Late at night when humans snore in the rooms above, the Brownies bake tasty breads and tiny biscuits to sell at the fairy market.

Animal Friends

~ ✧ ~

Flower Fairies share their woodland, garden, meadow and
wayside homes with many small creatures. Naturally gentle and good,
Flower Fairies have many friends in the animal kingdom with whom they
cooperate in times of need. A special favourite with animals, the kind
Self-Heal Fairy uses her herb to cure creatures when they fall ill. Animals
and Flower Fairies can understand each other when they talk
and rely heavily upon each other. Not all animals assist the fairies, though.
Greenflies sap juices from leaves, beetles munch petals and ants burrow
around plants' roots. Flower Fairies do not wish these pests any harm,
but they try to keep them away from their precious flowers.
Fortunately, ladybirds often help because they find the smallest
of these nuisances tasty!

Robins and blue tits help by eating the insects and caterpillars that destroy plants. In return for the fairies' berries and seeds, grateful birds trade their soft, downy feathers which make warm fairy beds. A mutual passion for music unites birds and fairies, and they often sing melodious duets that echo through the treetops.

Earthworms help the Flower Fairies by wriggling underground and carrying fresh soil to the flowers above. Toads also assist the Flower Fairies by dining on the slimy slugs that greedily chomp flowers. During the coldest months, shivering fairies huddle up against furry field mice to stay warm. Baby fairies straddle the mice and shriek with delight as they scurry through the fields. In exchange, the Flower Fairies gladly give their seeds and nuts for the timid mice to nibble.

The Winter Jasmine Fairy

Bees

~ ✧ ~

*B*ees carry pollen from flower to flower, which enables pollination to take place. Without bees, there would be no new flowers! Bees also collect flowers' nectar to make honey, the fairies' favourite sticky treat. When a bee comes buzzing by, the fairies gladly trade their flowers' nectar for a cup full of honey. The sweetest-smelling flowers attract the most bees. The fragrant *Red Clover Fairy* greets her insect visitors with a curtsy and obligingly invites them to sample red clover nectar. When the bees have filled their honeybags, she politely bows and urges them to visit again soon. Her cheery charm ensures a steady supply of honey for the Flower Fairies.

The RED CLOVER Fairy

Butterflies and Caterpillars

Butterflies, like bees, drink nectar from the insides of flowers and help to pollinate plants. Graceful butterflies flit alongside their friend the *Michaelmas Daisy Fairy*, playing merry games of chase and follow-my-leader.

They have an admiration of all beautiful things in common. Wherever there are flowers, there are sure to be butterflies. Some people even say that butterflies look like flowers with wings.

Although the Flower Fairies love butterflies, they are not fond of furry caterpillars. Hungry nearly all the time, these pesky little beasts munch big, gaping holes in leaves. This annoys the fairies who live in trees, as they do not want their leaves to look like Swiss cheese! The Flower Fairies long for the moment when a caterpillar sews its silky cocoon and emerges as their playmate, the butterfly.

Snails

~ ✳ ~

Whenever a snail appears, the fairies know that it will soon rain. After greeting his slow-moving friend and receiving a languid wave of the horns in reply, the *Ribwort Plantain Fairy* hurries into the undergrowth and forages for shelter. Snails do not worry about a downpour, for they can retreat into their shells. Flower Fairies collect empty snail shells and use them for furniture.

Grasshoppers

~ ✳ ~

*F*airy babies do not cry when they are put to bed in the evening,

for they hear grasshoppers and crickets chirping them a soothing lullaby.

Talkative, sociable creatures, grasshoppers enjoy chatting with the *Stork's-Bill*

Fairy for hours and hours. They challenge each other with riddles, tell silly jokes,

sing comic songs and whisper their deepest secrets.

Food

~ ·❋· ~

As many captives in fairyland would testify, humans should never, ever sample fairy food or drink. Even the smallest nibble could mean life imprisonment with no chance of escape, for all fairy food is spiced with magic. The culinary delicacies concocted by fairies prove difficult to resist, but humans should always politely decline an offer pleading a lack of appetite. Even if you managed to taste and escape, you would lose your palate for human food and soon waste away. Fairies have no scruples about eating human food. They are notorious for pilfering grain and milk from human kitchens, though they always return what they borrow. Do not be alarmed if you are missing a thimble-full of milk or a pinch of flour—consider it a fairy loan that will promptly be restored to your larder.

The Dog-Violet Fairy

56

Fairies have a terrible weakness for sweets. They crave sugary tastes and, though human sweets are inferior to fairy bonbons, you will certainly win elfin friends if you leave the occasional sweetmeat in the garden. (Of course, it is very likely that you will make ant friends as well!) Think twice before accusing someone of eating the last of your sweets, as the actual culprit might be a greedy little fairy. Each spring, the *Dog-Violet Fairy* candies some of his purple petals. These crystallized sweets are a delicious fairy treat and are often given as party favours at balls.

Honey is the fairies' favourite flavour, and they receive a plentiful supply from their friends the bees. Fairies drizzle honey over fruit and use it as a seasoning when they roast nuts. Sometimes, they dip their tiny fingers straight into the honey pot and lick off the sticky syrup. The bees often bring the fairies gifts of honeycomb, which they break into pieces and eat like sweets. The *Candytuft Fairy* gets her name because she makes delightful candies and sweet treats. Her speciality is scrumptious seed and honey candies so small that they would fit on your fingernail. Her confections are the highlight of fairy parties.

The Candytuft Fairy

Fruit

~ ☀ ~

$\mathcal{T}$hroughout the year, the Flower Fairies eat a

variety of juicy, sweet fruits. In the summertime,

the merry *Cherry Tree Fairy* harvests his ripe,

succulent cherries. The choicest cherries are

presented to the queen, then he offers the rest to the

The Cherry Tree Fairy

fairies and birds. The *Mulberry Fairy* invites the fairies to pick the

plump berries hanging off his tree's branches. The fairies stuff themselves full

of mulberries, until their fingers are stained purple. Summer also brings

raspberries, strawberries, blueberries and blackcurrents—which make luscious

meals for fairies. For special feasts the fairies concoct fruity puddings such

as magically light fairy fools and delicate cherry tarts

the size of a penny.

The Mulberry Fairy

58

Autumn brings a cornucopia of delicious fruit. The mischievous *Blackberry Fairy* teases the other fairies with thick clusters of black fruits hanging from prickly branches. The thorns scratch the fairies, but they hardly notice because they will dine on a feast of blackberries for dinner. With the extra berries that they collect, the Flower Fairies make bramble jam to eat on breads and cakes. Fairies welcome the first frost of the year because they know that soon the *Sloe Fairy* will announce that her plums are ready to eat. Some baby fairies, unable to resist the pretty purple fruits, disobey their elders and bite the sloes before they are ripe. They never make that mistake again, because sloes taste bitter and sharp until they have been mellowed by frost.

The Sloe
Fairy

*The Blackberry
Fairy*

WARNING: Flower Fairies are happy to share their fruit with humans, but there is one condition. Humans should never take nature's bounty for granted and should always leave enough fruit on the trees to feed the fairies. This precaution will keep the fairies content and ensure good harvests in the future.

$\mathcal{C}$rab-apples are rather tart for human tongues, but these little apples taste

just right for Flower Fairies. In September and October, crab-apple trees

become laden with fruit. The *Crab-Apple Fairy* makes jelly from her fruits

and shares it with all her friends. She also stews the bruised crab-apples that

have fallen to the ground and stores the sauce in acorn cups. The *Crab-Apple*

Fairy keeps the crab-apple preserve locked in a cupboard at the root of the

tree, so that the fairies will have food throughout the Winter.

During Autumn, fairies gather nuts that have ripened all Summer long. The Flower Fairies store these nuts to eat in cold months when food is scarce. They keep their stores of nuts in holes in trees, too small for squirrels and nuthatches to plunder. The impish *Sweet Chestnut Fairy* showers his shiny, fat nuts down from the highest branches, mischievously aiming for his friends' heads as he hides behind the golden leaves. No winter feast would be complete without roasted chestnuts as the main course.

Fairy Recipes

Dandelion Wine

Throughout Spring and Summer, the *Dandelion Fairy* collects his best blossoms and then ferments them to make wine. The Flower Fairies imbibe this exquisite drink only at very special events, such as fairy feasts and balls.

Dandelion Wine

4 dandelion heads   Plenty of fairy dust
8 acorn cups of dew

Leave acorn cups out on the grass overnight to collect dewdrops. Pour dew into a large vessel and add dandelion heads. Sprinkle a generous handful of fairy dust into the solution, then leave to ferment for a fortnight.

Autumn Medley

3 sweet chestnuts   1 fairy cheese
3 beechnuts   Crab-apple jelly

Remove nuts from shells, chop into tiny pieces, then roast in the sun for one day. When the nuts are warm, grate one fairy cheese and melt it over the nut mixture. Serve on a small birch leaf, with a bit of crab-apple preserve on the side.

The Beechnut Fairy's Autumn Medley

Though these quantities would not satisfy a human appetite, this savoury recipe feeds approximately six hungry fairies. Nobody cooks this dish quite like the *Beechnut Fairy*, who uses only the sweetest and ripest of her nuts.

The Hazel-Nut Fairy's Favourite Cake

This rich, decadent dessert, a traditional favourite at fairy celebrations, can be made with whatever fruit is in season. The *Hazel-Nut Fairy* refuses to divulge the secret ingredient, so this recipe is only an approximation.

Hazel-Nut Cake

Honey
Poppy seeds
1 cherry
1 strawberry

2 hazel-nuts
2 dewdrops
1 sprig of mint
Secret ingredient

Finely chop the fruit and hazel-nuts. Add a trickle of honey until the mixture is sticky, then scatter poppy seeds into the batter. Using a twig, stir in mint leaves and two dewdrops. Pour the batter into a kingcup flower and leave to set.

Flower Salad

1 marigold flower
2 nasturtium leaves
Sunflower seeds

1 stem of tansy
1 wild mushroom
Chive stems

Roughly tear the flower leaves, petals and stems. Mix the ingredients together in an empty horse chestnut shell. Sprinkle a smidgen of sunflower seeds and chopped chives over the salad before serving.

The Marigold Fairy's Flower Salad

Flower Fairies often toss colourful, nutritious salads made with the tasty leaves and petals growing in flower gardens. Many specimens of edible wild mushrooms and truffles grow in the woods, which fairies nibble for sustenance and add to their salads.

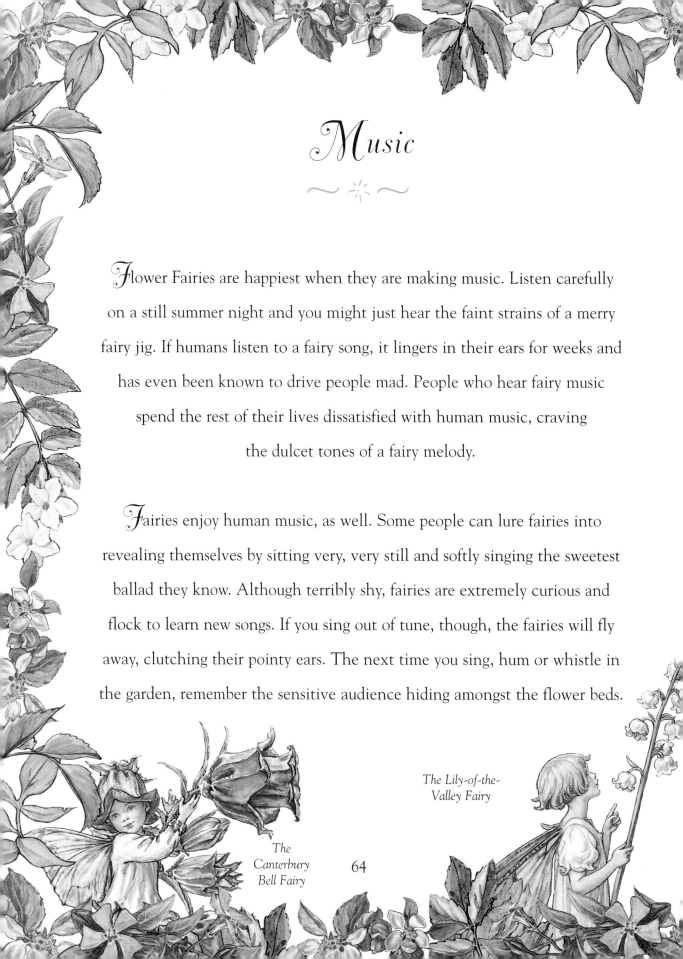

Music

Flower Fairies are happiest when they are making music. Listen carefully on a still summer night and you might just hear the faint strains of a merry fairy jig. If humans listen to a fairy song, it lingers in their ears for weeks and has even been known to drive people mad. People who hear fairy music spend the rest of their lives dissatisfied with human music, craving the dulcet tones of a fairy melody.

Fairies enjoy human music, as well. Some people can lure fairies into revealing themselves by sitting very, very still and softly singing the sweetest ballad they know. Although terribly shy, fairies are extremely curious and flock to learn new songs. If you sing out of tune, though, the fairies will fly away, clutching their pointy ears. The next time you sing, hum or whistle in the garden, remember the sensitive audience hiding amongst the flower beds.

The Lily-of-the-Valley Fairy

The Canterbury Bell Fairy

64

On warm summer nights, the *Canterbury Bell Fairy* sets his flowers swaying. Ding-dong-ding, the bells ring out over gardens and the countryside, calling the fairies to sing. The *Lily-of-the-Valley Fairy* tinkles her tiny, white bells in harmony with his deep chimes. When the fairies have gathered, the tattered *Ragged Robin Fairy* picks up his reed pipe and begins to play high, cheerful notes. The *Honeysuckle Fairy* blows on his trumpet, filling the air with joyous fanfare. Drawn to the irresistible sound, the fairies' animal friends join in with the fairy orchestra. Crickets and grasshoppers chirp melodiously like tiny violins. A chorus of toads croaks gently in the background. A family of rabbits taps its feet to the beat—thump, thump, thump.

The Ragged Robin Fairy

The Honeysuckle Fairy

Bugle

A brave sentinel, the *Bugle Fairy* stands at the edge of the woods, sounding his bugle when danger threatens the Flower Fairies. He gallantly fences hedgehogs with stalks of bluebell, fearlessly chases after dragonflies and tickles a grouchy fox with a blade of grass. When night falls, however, the *Bugle Fairy* joins the members of the fairy orchestra. A magically skilled musician, he plays deep, sonorous notes on his blue horn by moonlight.

The *Pear Blossom Fairy* enthusiastically leads the Flower Fairies' sing-alongs like a conductor. Possessing perfect pitch, he hums a note to get the fairy singers in tune. As the fairies sing their joyful songs, robins and wrens swoop down to trill along with the fairy chorus. From his treetop perch, the *Pear Blossom Fairy* cries with delight, "Sing, sing, sing you blackbirds! Sing, you beautiful thrush!" and waves his hands in time with the music.

Dance

~ ✳ ~

Have you ever noticed strange circular patches of grass surrounded by toadstools? Can you guess what they are? Those circles are fairy rings, where hundreds of tiny feet have trampled the night before while you were sound asleep. The toadstools enclose the fairies' revelry, as they dance under the light of the moon. If you hunt for fairy rings early in the morning, look carefully through the crushed grass and underneath toadstools—you might find a tiny shoe that a fairy dancer left behind!

It is impossible to resist the fairy orchestra's music. When the musicians strike up a tune, the *Almond Blossom Fairy* and the *Cowslip Fairy* gleefully lead the Flower Fairies into the circle. Holding a pink bough in her hand, the *Almond Blossom Fairy* urges the fairies to join hands. Round and round they dance, spinning wildly and laughing giddily.

The Cowslip Fairy

Sometimes the fairies dance in a line, clapping and stomping their feet. If music is playing and no other fairies can be found, a Flower Fairy will happily twist and whirl in a solitary dance.

Fairies can dance without tiring until dawn, never once stopping to catch their breath. Humans have occasionally been drawn into fairy circles by the intoxicating music and the tinkling laughter. The consequences are always grim. Because one night in fairy time can equal weeks in human time, the capering never seems to cease. A human dancing with fairies inevitably wastes away, having no rest or food for many nights and days on end.

The Almond Blossom Fairy

> ## Invitation to the Summer Ball
>
> ⁓ ✴ ⁓
>
> *The Garden Fairies cordially invite you to a celebration of Summer.*
> *The evening will feature a dance recital starring the Fuchsia Fairy.*
> *Where: The Fairy Circle*
> *When: Midnight, Full Moon in July*
> *Please R.S.V.P.*

The most splendid fairy dancing happens at balls. When a community of Flower Fairies hosts a ball, they write out invitations on silvery slips of birch bark using ink made from berries and pine needle pens. All the Flower Fairies are invited, from the lowliest weed fairy to the loftiest tree fairy. For the Summer Ball, the *Pink Fairies* use their special scissors to make garlands and decorations from flower petals to adorn the fairy dell. They strew the remaining triangles of petal over the grassy fairy circle. The *Laburnum Fairy* contributes her showers of golden flowers,

The Pink Fairies

70

which hang overhead like streamers. The *Jasmine Fairy* places bouquets of glimmering white jasmine all around the bower to scent the night air with their sweet fragrance.

The Laburnum Fairy

At last, the long-awaited evening has arrived! A full moon illuminates the starry sky, casting a soft glow over the circle of spotted toadstools. Fireflies flit around the circle and light up the night like tiny, flickering lanterns. Glow-worms shine a warm, greenish light. At the stroke of midnight, excited Flower Fairies file into the fairy circle wearing their party finery spangled with dew. The fairy fiddlers and pipers tune their instruments as the guests mingle, nibble cakes and sip wine. The highlight of the evening is the midnight dance recital. For this special display, the very best fairy dancers have practised their routines for weeks and weeks.

The Jasmine Fairy

71

The little *Bird's-Foot Trefoil Fairy* performs first. Grasshoppers chirp
a lively tune and hoppetty hop the fairy is off! This is her very first ball
and she is up well past her bedtime, but she does not make one mistake.
Hop! Skip! Jump! Concentrating hard, she prances around the fairy ring on
her chubby, nimble legs to the country reel. The Flower Fairies cheer her
with a big round of applause to praise her debut performance.

A drum roll sounds and a hush falls over the crowd as the bright
Crocus Fairies take the stage. Faster and faster they cavort,
until they become a dazzling blur of colour. Round and round they
whirl as the audience marvels at their dizzying speed! As the music
crescendos, the *Crocus Fairies* clap their hands in time to
the beat and urge the audience to clap along.

Columbine

*N*ext to dance is the *Columbine Fairy*. As an elf tootles a solo on his pipe, she holds her skirts out and delicately twirls to the rhythm. Her light feet, shod in dainty slippers, move so quickly that they don't seem to touch the ground. She leaps and spins around the fairy ring, a blaze of pink and yellow. With a final pirouette, the blushing *Columbine Fairy* curtsies modestly and flutters off the stage.

Fuchsia

For the grand finale, the *Fuchsia Fairy*, dressed in a frilly purple and red tutu, tiptoes confidently on to the stage. The fairy orchestra plays slow, dreamy music while the *Fuchsia Fairy* gracefully executes her ballet steps and turns. The moon casts a beam like a spotlight on her elegant arabesques, jetés and plies. When the *Fuchsia Fairy* takes her bow, the Flower Fairies give her a long standing ovation.

Fun and Games

~ ✳ ~

The Silver Birch Fairy

Although numerous duties keep the Flower Fairies busy, they always find plenty of time for fun. Fairies are not competitive creatures and any fairy that wishes to play can join in the game. They care less about winning than they do about enjoying themselves as they play. Cheating is unheard of in the fairy world, as they value honesty above all other traits.

The Flower Fairies gambol through the fields and forests, using nature as a giant playground. Long, twining stems of bindweed and fine stems of harebell make ideal skipping ropes for fairies, who hop and jump while chanting rhyming songs. Fairies who live in trees have their very own swings. They perch upon slender branches and let the wind blow them back and forth. The more daring fairies dangle recklessly from the branches and sway in the breeze.

The Alder Fairy

Fairies never tire of challenging the butterflies to races. A furious fluttering of wings ensues as they fly from one end of a garden to the other.

The oldest and most popular fairy sport is called hurling. Those who have witnessed a hurling match report that it resembles the human game of cricket. Two teams play the game on a flat, grassy clearing with tall flowers to mark each end of the playing field. Using a twig as a bat, the players hit a cherry stone and then sprint or fly between the two posts. During the match, music accompanies the playing. Throughout Summer, hurling matches occur between different communities of fairies. The outcome of the game, however, is less important than the lively party after the match. In fact, the players will often forget to keep score and be unsure which team has won.

The Ash Tree
Fairy

$\mathcal{F}$lower Fairies love to play hide-and-seek. Countless hiding places lurk in the undergrowth: inside bell-shaped flowers, underneath ferns and high in the treetops. The *Elder Fairy* searches high and low for her friends. Some fairies disguise themselves amongst bunches of flowers, but the agile *Ash Tree Fairy* tiptoes to hide behind the loftiest leaves. If the *Elder Fairy* has difficulty detecting them, the hidden fairies sing to help her track them down.

$\mathcal{F}$lower Fairies scratch hopscotch grids into the dry earth with twigs. Jumping from square to square keeps the fairies warm and happy in Winter. Hard, red holly berries make perfect marbles for fairies. Peer under a holly bush and you might discover a giggling group of fairies lying on their tummies, flicking berries into a circle drawn in the soil. The Flower Fairies always greet the first snowfall of the year with delight. They run to find old, dried leaves and use them as toboggans to slide down snowy hills.

The Elder Fairy

78

*The Pine Tree
Fairy*

$\mathcal{T}$he *Gorse Fairies* play kiss chase with the other fairies, running through meadows and tagging them with a quick peck on the lips. The *Heather Fairy* swiftly flees their clutches—he doesn't want a kiss! Other fairies entertain themselves by playing a version of ninepins. They set up nine pine cones in a triangular formation and then roll shiny horse chestnuts to knock them down. Remember, a chestnut is as heavy as a bowling ball if you are a tiny fairy. Mischievous Flower Fairies tease squirrels by throwing down nuts from the treetops and aiming for their bushy tails. Playing pranks on humans is also a favourite fairy pastime. A falling horse chestnut or pine cone that lands on your head may not be an accident!

The Heather Fairy

*The Gorse
Fairies*

79

Spring

~ ✦ ~

Fairies do not need calendars to tell the date or time. Instead, they look for signs from nature. Each year, around 20th March, the Vernal Equinox occurs. As the days grow longer, spring flowers begin to bloom. The *Tulip Fairy* is an early riser. She gently wakes up her tulip bulbs and encourages them to poke their sleepy heads out of the cold, hard soil. Even though the winds still feel chilly, the Flower Fairies know that Spring has arrived when the first tulip shoots emerge from the ground.

At noon on 11th May, the Flower Fairies gather for the Spring Fling, a joyous festival of nature and rebirth. Wearing their best, brightest clothes, they festoon the *Tulip Fairy* with crowns and garlands. The *Tulip Fairy* stands at the centre of a grassy circle and presides over the festivities as the other fairies lay posies of may flowers and wild cherry blossoms at her feet. As a chorus of robins and wrens warbles a lively song, the fairies skip around the *Tulip Fairy*. The human tradition of dancing around a May Pole derives from this fairy ceremony.

Summer

~ ✳ ~

At daybreak on 21st June, the four day Summer Solstice Celebration
begins. Around this time, you might notice that your garden looks
rather overgrown. This is because, hooray, the Flower Fairies are taking their
annual holiday! The Flower Fairies abandon their chores, attend wonderful
parties and compete in the annual hurling championship. When the game
finishes, the fairies picnic along the sides of the field, munching a luscious
banquet of fruit and cakes. After lunch, the Flower Fairies sunbathe, nap in
the shade or wade in a nearby stream until the next party.

The merriment climaxes at the gala Midsummer's Night Ball,
held on 24th June in the *Lime Tree Fairy*'s bower. If you should wander
outdoors on Midsummer's Night, keep your ears and eyes open.
This is the one night of the year when all humans can see fairies.
Fear not if you see them revelling, for you will suffer no harm.

Autumn

~ ✳ ~

*W*hen leaves turn from green to dazzling shades of gold and red, when the days get shorter and chillier, and when nature bursts with plenty, the Flower Fairies sense that Autumn has come. On 22nd September, the evening of the Autumn Equinox, the Flower Fairies celebrate the Harvest Moon Festival. By the glowing light of a full moon, the fairies gather in a wheat field for a lavish feast of seasonal dishes. Before they eat, the *Hawthorn Fairy* solemnly pours a libation of cowslip wine into the soil. This thanksgiving ceremony ensures a bountiful harvest. Farmers should be especially considerate to Flower Fairies at harvest time, as the success of their crops depends on the fairies' intervention.

*T*he Flower Fairies sew ornate costumes for the raucous masquerade ball on All Hallow's Eve. At midnight the fairies convene around a crackling bonfire and reveal their true identities. On this day of the year, humans may find themselves the victims of pixie pranks and fairy tricks.

Winter

Winter brings cold, grey days, shimmering icicles and fluffy mounds of snow. Although it may look as though plant life has gone into hibernation, the Flower Fairies carefully tend the evergreens, such as pine and box, and brush heavy snow off fragile shrubs to prevent damage.

The Winter Solstice occurs on 22nd December. On that night, the *Christmas Tree Fairy* waves her glittering wand and leads a torch-lit procession to the Winter Wonderland Carnival. The fairies weave through the woodlands underneath the shelter of fir trees, carolling as they walk. The waxy, red berries of the yew trees glow like candles, lighting up a path through the dark undergrowth. At the carnival, the fairies skate over slippery puddles, build Snow-Fairies and drink steaming cups of sweet peppermint tea to stay warm. The youngest fairies dash about throwing snowballs the size of peas and playing kiss chase with sprigs of mistletoe.

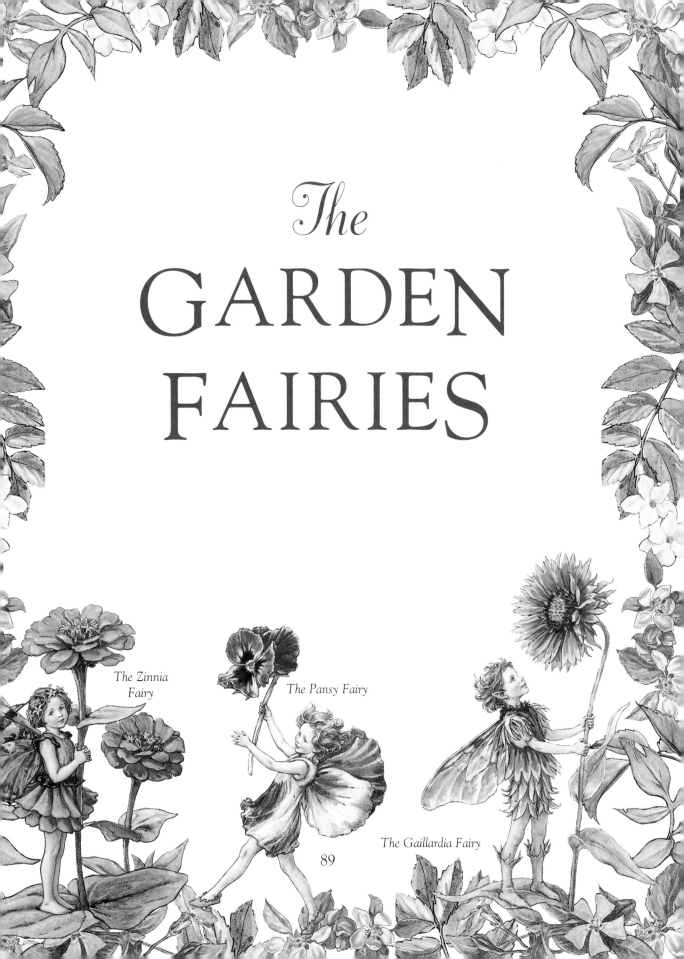

The
GARDEN
FAIRIES

The Zinnia
Fairy

The Pansy Fairy

The Gaillardia Fairy

The Polyanthus and Grape Hyacinth Fairies

The *Polyanthus and Grape Hyacinth Fairies* wake up at dawn, stretching and yawning and greeting one another. These exuberant little fairies live in sociable clusters at ground level on flower bed edges. Cheerful chatterboxes, they keep the whole garden informed of all comings and goings. After a busy day of gossiping they fall asleep together in a cosy dormitory tucked between the edge of the flower bed and the lawn, hidden by the overhanging blades of grass and sheltered by glossy leaves. If you lift up a leaf you might spy the slumbering fairies still mumbling and wriggling in their sleep. Ssh! Don't wake them up.

*O*nce upon a time, the *Cornflower Fairy* lived in a field, surrounded by red poppies and golden sheaves of corn. Now people plant his beautiful flowers in formal flower beds, amongst the elegant lilies and roses. The *Cornflower Fairy* skips and bounds merrily around the lawn and borders, admiring his delicate neighbours who teasingly call him "Boy Blue". This simple country lad needs to pinch himself to believe that he is now a stylish garden fairy!

The *Geranium Fairy* lives in an earthen flowerpot near the garden steps.
During hot summer days, she naps peacefully against the cool edge of the
pot, under the shade of a geranium leaf. At dusk, she flies from windowbox
to hanging basket, keeping the soil watered and plucking off wilted leaves.
Some fairies wonder that the *Geranium Fairy* doesn't find her pot confining
and lonely, but she dwells contentedly in her own, private little home.

93

The Rose Fairy

If you sit quietly in the gathering gloom of the evening,

listen for a hushed, whispering sound that seems to come from near

the garden wall. This is not the evening breeze, it is the gentle voice of the

Rose Fairy. Like a mother to all the garden fairies, she reminds naughty little

fairies that others would like to get some sleep, as they must wake up before

dawn. Roses are the pride and joy of many a gardener, but their rose

bushes look lovely because the industrious *Rose Fairy* spends daybreak

busily tending to the pink and red flowers. To make sure that

people don't carelessly pluck her exquisite blossoms, the *Rose Fairy*

sharpens her flowers' thorns in self-defence.

The garden fairies nicknamed the *Heliotrope Fairy* "Cherry Pie". Can you

guess why? Just stroll through your garden when her rich, purple flowers are

in bloom and soon you can tell—the *Heliotrope Fairy* perfumes the garden

with a delicious smell. She invites the other fairies to sit under her scented

blossoms and daydream about the sweet treats that they love to eat.

Follow your nose and you might catch the garden fairies napping, their

tiny noses sniffing the fragranced air.

Wallflower

*T*he *Wallflower Fairy* sits on the garden wall, of course. He perches in his velvety finery on a cushion of moss, with clusters of his fragrant flowers growing from every nook and cranny in the stone. This shy little fairy has the best view of the whole garden and can wave to all his friends. Why are people who don't join in dancing sometimes called wallflowers? Because even at the liveliest balls, the *Wallflower Fairy* prefers to watch the revelry from the wall, nodding his head and tapping his toes along to the music.

One of the busiest garden fairies is the *Shirley Poppy Fairy*. This frilly pink fairy never rests. She spends her days skipping and spinning through the grass, gleefully shaking wee black seeds from seed-heads that look like pepper-pots. Flitting around the garden on her nimble toes, she cries, "Go, sleep, and awaken like me!" She hopes that the ripe seeds will fall deep in the soil and grow next year, bringing more *Shirley Poppy Fairies* to help her.

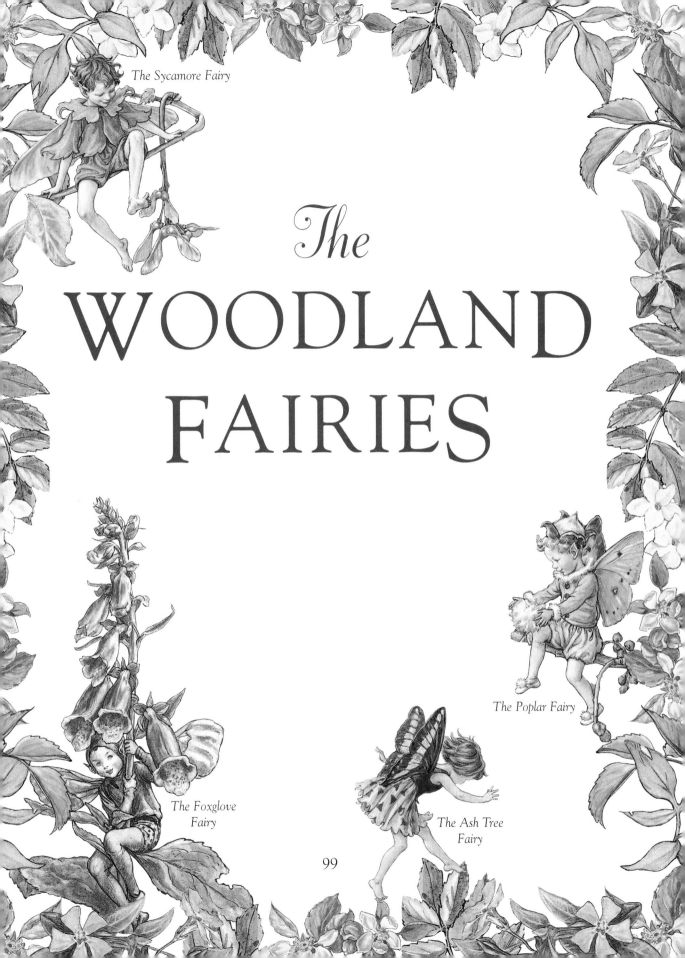

The Sycamore Fairy

The
WOODLAND
FAIRIES

The Poplar Fairy

The Foxglove
Fairy

The Ash Tree
Fairy

The Elm Tree Fairy

At the edge of the woods grows a row of stately elm trees inhabited by a little elf. Perched on a stumpy bough and concealed by a mass of soft, green leaves, the *Elm Tree Fairy* overlooks the fields and country lanes. If visitors wander into the woods, the *Elm Tree Fairy* alerts his woodland friends to keep watch over them. It is all too easy to go astray in the dark woods, and the good Flower Fairies dwelling in the treetops helpfully guide lost creatures back to safety. At night flocks of larks and rooks fly home to roost in the loftiest elm boughs. "Goodnight," they chirp, as the *Elm Tree Fairy* whistles on his way to a midnight fairy fête.

The Bluebell Fairy.

*W*here the great oaks and beeches meet in a leafy bower lies the cool, lush Woodland Court. Overhead, thrushes sing majestic fanfare in praise of the peerless Woodland King. Amidst a splendid carpet of sapphire flowers, the *Bluebell Fairy* reigns fairly over the woods. He holds a tall, straight stem of bluebells as a sceptre and commands respect from all his woodland subjects; even the sternest owls and the most impertinent elves pay him homage.

The Primrose Fairy.

*B*eside the *Bluebell Fairy* sits his queen, the lovely *Primrose Fairy*.
Surrounded by a bevy of maids, she possesses the grace and dignity befitting
the Woodland Queen. Her attendants comb her pale hair with a sprig of
pine and offer her acorn cups of nectar. When the woodland fairies come to
the court bearing gifts of musky perfume and succulent berries, the *Primrose
Fairy* rewards them with a radiant smile and sincere thanks.

The Ground Ivy Fairy

~ ⁍ ~

The tiny *Ground Ivy Fairy* darts over the damp, mossy ground around the roots of the trees. He has only just left the fairy school and taken responsibility for his pretty, purple plants. This is his very first Spring and there are so many purple flowers to look after. It seems as though every time he turns his head a new flower crops up, creeping and spreading over the forest floor. His work never seems to end. The *Ground Ivy Fairy* scrambles after all of his plants, panting with exhaustion as he tries to keep track of them. Fortunately, his kind friends in the treetops above call down advice and encouragement. "Don't fret," they say. "Every Flower Fairy finds his job difficult at first!"

The *Nightshade Fairy* has an onerous duty, for his flowers contain poison.
The *Nightshade Fairy* must protect the other woodland fairies and humans
from sampling his berries and touching his flowers. If you wander too close to
his climbing plant, you will hear him hiss an urgent warning in your ear.
Though his flowers are pretty purple and yellow, the *Nightshade Fairy* lurks in
damp shadows and hides behind other plants to avoid attracting attention.

The *Nightshade Berry Fairy* plays a dangerous game with his deadly berries. He coyly tempts the other fairies with the gleaming ruby berries in Autumn. Feigning innocence, he dangles the bright berries alluringly and asks, "Why should you think my berries poisoned things?" The good *Nightshade Fairy* quickly chases his neighbour and enemy away, but so long as the branches are laden with berries, the *Nightshade Berry Fairy* will work his fatal mischief.

As you venture deeper into the woods a grove of beech trees looms. With their smooth, grey trunks, the trees look like stone pillars. On a branch high above the ground lounges the *Beech Tree Fairy*, who ensures that all the beeches in the woods stay healthy from their thick, mossy roots to their tallest limbs. During Spring, he lovingly combs the silky fringe that hangs from each new, green leaf. Round, green balls dangle from each twig and will become prickly beechnut shells in Autumn.

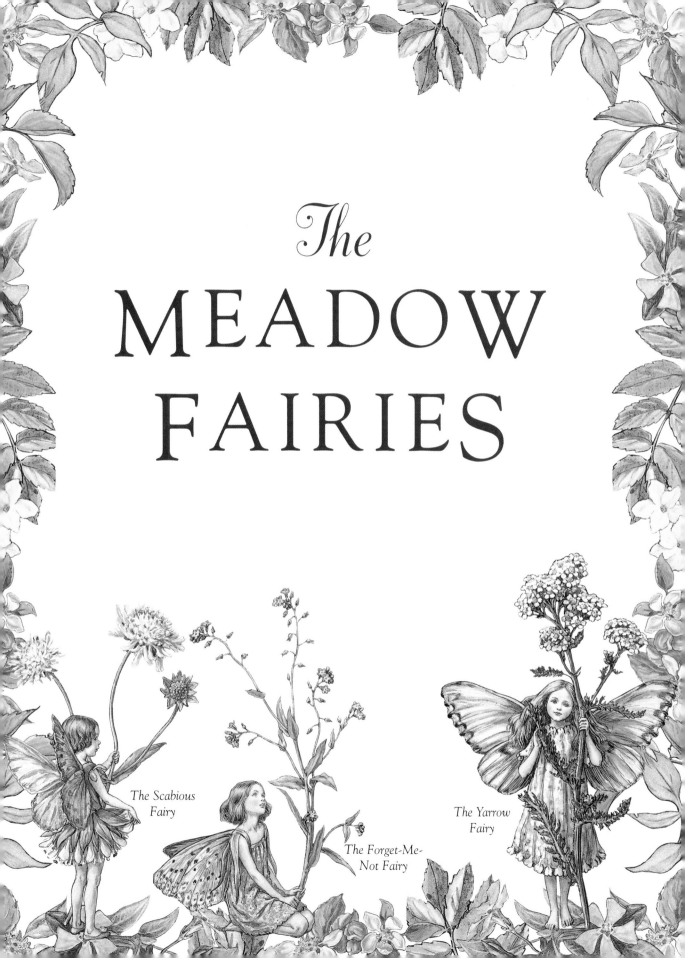

The
MEADOW
FAIRIES

The Scabious
Fairy

The Forget-Me-
Not Fairy

The Yarrow
Fairy

The Daisy Fairy

~ ☀ ~

The *Daisy Fairy* weaves daisy chains to drape around the necks of the fluffy lambs and awkward colts who graze in the meadow where she lives. The animals' necklaces do not go uneaten for long! Unlike some mischievous meadow fairies, the *Daisy Fairy* never teases the cows by pretending to be a buzzing fly. Because she is still young and needs lots of rest, the *Daisy Fairy* bids goodnight to the other Flower Fairies at dusk. She tenderly folds down her tiny flowers' red and white petals at sunset. Having tucked in her flowers, she curls up in her snug bed of grass. When the *Daisy Fairy* awakes with the morning sunshine, she opens up her flowers' petals and looks eagerly for animal playmates in the pasture.

The Daisy Fairy.

As Summer reaches its prime, yellow ragwort sprouts along grassy country ways. Ragwort might only be a humble weed, but the *Ragwort Fairy* prizes her sunny flowers and tends them as if they were made from gold. A bold country lass, the *Ragwort Fairy* gleefully wriggles her bare feet in the freshly tilled soil and fearlessly tumbles down grassy hills. Too tomboyish to rehearse dance steps or play demure games, the *Ragwort Fairy* tickles other fairies with a tassel of corn silk and uses a tall blade of grass as a skipping rope.

Eyebright

Take care where you tread on country paths, or you might step on the *Eyebright Fairy*. You need bright eyes to see eyebright, for its flowers are very, very tiny. Though small and meek, the *Eyebright Fairy* does not hide in a sheltered nook. He lives on the bare, open hillside with the turf as his carpet and the sky as his roof. Rabbits find eyebright irresistible and nuzzle the *Eyebright Fairy* as they nibble stalks of his flowers. The little fairy giggles as the rabbits' pink, twitching noses tickle his toes.

The Poppy Fairy

The glorious, raven-haired *Poppy Fairy* resides in wheat fields, amongst the golden sheaves. She works together with the scarecrows to protect the grain from plundering birds. From when the wheat is young and green to when it grows ripe and plump, she scolds the greedy crows when they eat too much. The larks always respect the *Poppy Fairy*'s wishes, and chirp along with her lovely soprano voice as she flutters through the fields doing her chores. When the harvest ends, she twirls through the bare fields with her silky, red skirts billowing in the breeze. As the *Poppy Fairy* dances through the ploughed rows, she scatters her tiny black seeds into the soil to plant a crop of crimson poppies for the following year.

*B*right red flowers border dry, dusty lanes all over the countryside in Summer. Enquire what these cheerful blooms are called and you might be told Robin-in-the-Hedge, Red Jack, Soldier's Buttons or even Robin Hood! The elusive fairy who looks after these flowers with many aliases knows that their real name is red campion, for he is the *Red Campion Fairy*. Dressed in scarlet from head to pointy toes, he sits so still upon a leaf that ramblers walking through the meadow mistake him for one of his flowers.

*A*nother Flower Fairy with a secret lives in grassy meadows.

The *Bee Orchis Fairy* dresses in a velvety brown tunic and a pink, horned hat. He proudly guards a green stem with hungry bees feasting on the pink flowers' nectar. Look how still the bees are as they work. Why, those aren't bees! They're flowers that look like bees! The *Bee Orchis Fairy*, camouflaged by his clothes, giggles impishly at your mistake. Though the bee orchis does not buzz and does not sting, you must never pick the flower for it is very rare.

The *Scarlet Pimpernel Fairy* lies on his back peering up at the clouds above. When fairies need to predict the weather, they seek out the *Scarlet Pimpernel Fairy*. He uses his plant as a fairy weatherglass to tell whether the day will be sunny or gloomy. If the red flowers are open, the fairies expect a warm, bright day. When the flowers stay tightly shut, the fairies prepare for rain. You, too, can search for the fairy weatherman along country lanes.

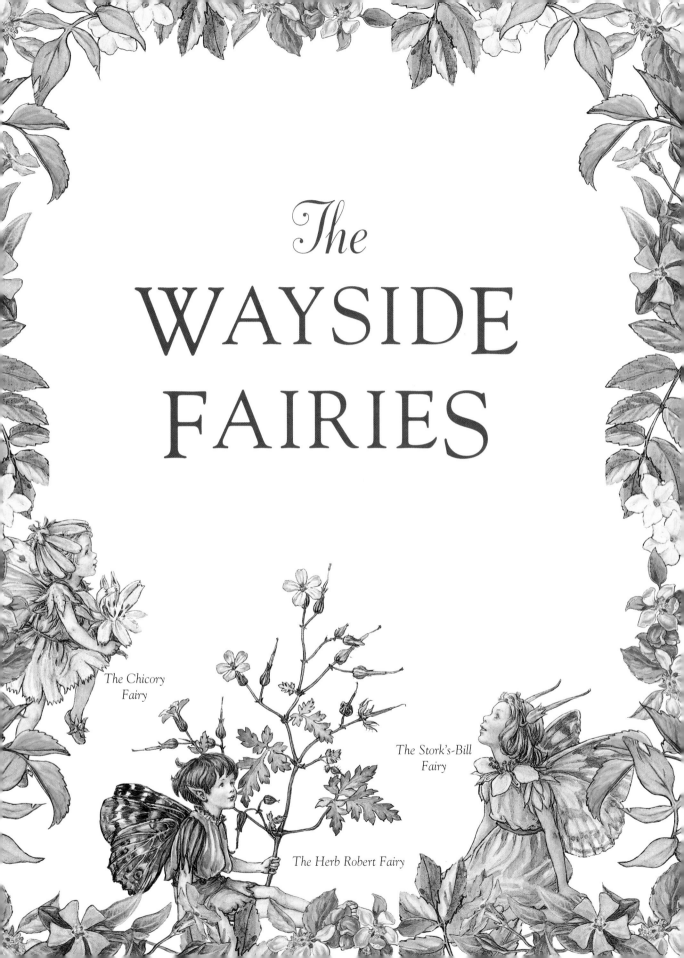

The
WAYSIDE
FAIRIES

The Chicory
Fairy

The Stork's-Bill
Fairy

The Herb Robert Fairy

The White Bindweed Fairy

~ ⋇ ~

Long stems of white bindweed twine along the wayside, decorating hedges and roadsides with garlands of pure white trumpets. Though she looks mild and innocent, you would not wish to invite the *White Bindweed Fairy* to come and live in your garden. As it rapidly grows, white bindweed winds around other plants and trees in a very persistent manner. Some people even call white bindweed the "Hedge Strangler". Like her beautiful bell-shaped flowers, the *White Bindweed Fairy* can be very stubborn. When deciding which game to play or which song to sing, she sulks if she cannot have her own way. Fortunately, the *White Bindweed Fairy* has impeccable taste and the other fairies usually agree with her choice.

A dauntless rogue, the *Sow Thistle Fairy* spreads his weeds wherever they

are not wanted. He never asks permission before urging his seeds to "Go fly!"

A cheeky chap who delights in making mischief, he flaunts his yellow

flowers in wasteland and sneaks them into hedgerows. You can try to drive

out his weeds with spades, but this tousle-haired fairy does not lack

determination and will soon trespass again!

*A*nother naughty fairy, the *Burdock Fairy* gleefully torments people passing

by the roadsides and hedgerows where his little brown burrs grow. These

burrs cling tenaciously to skirts, trousers and stockings. The *Burdock Fairy*

giggles and mocks as his frustrated victims try to unstick the prickly burrs.

Though rather troublesome, the *Burdock Fairy* means no harm.

He simply cannot resist a good laugh!

123

The Rose-Bay Willow-Herb Fairy

The *Rose-Bay Willow-Herb Fairy* has no regard for airs and graces. Where other fairies would sniff and turn their noses up in disdain, the *Rose-Bay Willow-Herb Fairy* gladly sets up home. The most open and welcoming of all the Flower Fairies, she brightens up forlorn places and neglected spaces with a blanket of bright pink blossoms. She brings a burst of colour to earth that has been burnt and singed by forest fires. Her flowers are beacons of hope in scenes of ruin and despair. When she has settled in, the *Rose-Bay Willow-Herb Fairy* lets the breeze carry her flowers' fluffy seeds to other needy places. Her charity extends to fairies and humans, as well. She flies to rescue any struggling Flower Fairy and takes pity on troubled humans, sometimes even granting their wishes!

Thrift

*F*ew wanderers come her way, so the *Thrift Fairy* takes no pains to hide.
Even sure-footed sheep do not venture to the edge of the steep cliffs where
her pink flowers grow. Spilling from every crevice and chink in the rock, her
rosy blooms flourish undisturbed above the sparkling blue sea. From her
towering precipice, the *Thrift Fairy* waves to the seagulls flying overhead and
gazes down at the crashing waves. She dances along the rock-face under the
azure sky, never afraid of losing her balance.

The *Horned Poppy Fairy* inhales a deep breath of salty sea air, bracing

himself against the coastal breeze and the sea's foamy spray. His marvellous

horned flowers grow along the pebbly beach. Watching the boats sailing by,

he dreams of being a mariner and imagines adventures on the high seas.

The *Horned Poppy Fairy* flies to the sea and dips his fingers in the frothy

waves. Chilled by the icy water, he glances fondly behind him at the dry

sand dunes and decides to stay safe in his seashore home.